NEW BIG FUN 1

Student's Book and eBook

Mario Herrera • Barbara Hojel

New Big Fun Student's Book 1

Pearson Education Limited
KAO Two, KAO Park, Hockham Way, Harlow, CM17 9SR. England
and Associated Companies throughout the world.
www.pearsonenglish.com/bigfun

First published 2018
ISBN: 978-1-292-39290-5
Set in Gill Sans Infant Std
Printed in China (GCC/01)

Artwork/Photo Acknowledgements
Page 1 (boy) AJP/Shutterstock, (crayon) Cara Purdy/Shutterstock;(puppet) Tania Zbrodko/ Shutterstock; (paper) Irina Nartova/Shutterstock; (shelf) Andrea Crisante/123RF.com; p. 2 (top) Maria Pia Marrella/Pearson, (middle) Alex James Bramwell/ Shutterstock, (bottom) VenusAngel/ Shutterstock; p. 3 (top) Cara Purdy/Shutterstock, (middle) Nikolai Artiushkin/123RF.com, (bottom) Photobac/Shutterstock; p. 12 (background) Artens/Shutterstock, (left) Ionia/Shutterstock, (middle) hwongcc/Shutterstock, (right) irin-k/Shutterstock; p. 15 Design Pics Inc./ Alamy; p. 16 (top) Stephanie Frey/ Shutterstock, (middle) Stephanie Frey/Shutterstock, (bottom) Stephanie Frey/Shutterstock; p. 17 Harm Kruyshaar/Shutterstock; p. 20 (Left) 2xSamara/ Shutterstock, (Upper Right) 2xSamara/ Shutterstock, (Lower Right) Goran Bogicevic/Shutterstock; p. 21 (Lower Left) Butterfly Hunter/ Shutterstock; p. 26 (background) Artens/Shutterstock, (left) thka/Shutterstock, (right) Yavus Meyveci/Shutterstock; (Lower Right) Pavel Timofeev/123RF p. 27 Sergiy Bykhunenko/Shutterstock; p. 28 (left 3) Stephanie Frey/Shutterstock, (right 3) Harm Kruyshaar/Shutterstock; p. 29 KyuOh/Getty Images; p. 30 (top) Andrey Arkusha/ Shutterstock, (middle) Kurhan/Shutterstock, (bottom) Heather LaVelle/ Shutterstock; p. 31 (top) Supri Suharjoto/Shutterstock, (middle) Kenishirotie/Shutterstock, (bottom) wong sze yuen/Shutterstock; TERTFp. 40 (background) blickwinkel/Alamy, (left) Pat Thielen/Alamy, (bottom) Alison Thompson/Alamy; p. 41 Phase4Photography/ Shutterstock; p. 43 (left) Oksana Kuzmina/Shutterstock, (middle left) graja/Shutterstock, (middle right) Olgysha/ Shutterstock, (right) mates/ Fotolia; p. 44 (top) Cheuk-king Lo/Pe arson Education Asia Ltd, (middle) graja/Shutterstock, (bottom) Diana Taliun/123RF.com; p. 45 (top) fotos_v/Shutterstock, (middle) LungLee/Shutterstock, (bottom) Birgit Reitz-Hofmann/Shutterstock; p. 48 (upper left) LeManna/Shutterstock, (lower left) Tamara Kulikova/Shutterstock, (upper right) Rawpixel.Icom/Shutterstock, (lower right) Artazum/ Shutterstock; p. 54 Sergey Novikov/ 123RF, (bottom) vita khorzhevska/Shutterstock; p. 55 Andrey Arkusha/Shutterstock; p. 59 Vanessa Davies/DK Images, (cookie) Richard Villalon/Fotolia; p. 57 kazoka/Shutterstock (cookie) Nattika/Shutterstock; p. 58 (top) Brent Hofacker/Shutterstock, (middle) Odua Images/Shutterstock, (bottom) Terry Leung/Pearson Education Asia Ltd; p. 59 (top) HandmadePictures/Shutterstock, (middle) HomeStudio/Shutterstock, (bottom) OduaImages/Fotolia; p. 68 (left) Kostiantyn Ablazov/Shutterstock, Anna Kucherova/Shutterstock (Right) andregric/Shutterstock, HomeStudio/Shutterstock; p. 69 (left) Purestock/Alamy, (right) majesticca/Istock/Getty Images; p. 71 Florian Schott/Shutterstock; p. 72 (top) Irina Rogov/ Shutterstock, (middle) maxstockphoto/Shutterstock, (bottom) Ruslan Kudrin/Shutterstock; p. 73 (top) Elnur/ Shutterstock, (middle) Trevor Clifford/Pearson Education Ltd, (bottom) Karkas/ Shutterstock; p. 82 Dann Tardif/LWA/Corbis/Glow Images, (bottom left) Erik Nuenighoff/Shutterstock,(bottom middle) A3pfamily/Shutterstock; p. 83 Rob Marmion/Shutterstock; p. 85 Lana K/ Shutterstock (fish) dibrova/Shutterstock (kitten) Elya Vatel/Shutterstock; p. 86 (top) haveseen/Shutterstock, (middle) thumb/Shutterstock, (bottom) Mi.Ti./Shutterstock; p. 87 (top) Radomir Rezny/Shutterstock, (middle) Miroslav Hlavko/Shutterstock, (bottom) Elya Vatel/Shutterstock; p. 96 (background) PHOTO FUN/Shutterstock, (left) Eric Isselee/Shutterstock, (middle) whitaker/ Shutterstock, (right) PHOTO FUN/Shutterstock; p. 97 KidStock/Alamy; p. 99 (left) Paulaphoto /Shutterstock; (left) Gelpi JM/Shutterstock, (right) Comstock Images/Getty Images; p. 100 (top) gwimages/Shutterstock, (middle) Hugh Sitton/Corbis/Getty Images, (bottom) Michael Folmer/Alamy; p. 101 (top) Lucky Business/Shutterstock, (middle) Goodluz/ Shutterstock, (bottom) Jacob Wakerhausen/E+/Getty Images; p. 110 (left, middle, right) Emilia Stasiak/Shutterstock, (bottom left) kiyanochka1/Shutterstock, (bottom right) Mazimilian Lange/123RF; p. 111 Jamie Grill/Blend Images/Getty Images; p. 113 KidStock/Blend Images/Getty Images; p. 114 Zoroyan/Shutterstock; p. 115 serrnovik/Shutterstock

Music credits
Music composed by John Farrell, Hope River Music, www.johnfarrell.net, and Jeff Miller, Grant's Corners, Walden, NY, assisted by Conway Chewning. Music and vocal recordings produced by Jeff Miller and John Farrell. Recorded and mixed by Jeff Miller at Grant's Corners, Remote Recordings, Yorktown Heights, NY, and Hillsdale, NY. Song lyrics by Barbara Hojel, with contributions by John Farrell. Children's vocal performance directed by Lorraine Cich. Child vocal performers: Julia Apostolou, Aisha Bhakta, Emma Halderman, Cassidy Kenney, Juliana Moscati; adult vocal performers: Lorraine Cich, John Farrell, Maggie Farrell, Ann Marie Lord. Edit: Eastern Sky Media Services, Inc. Casselberry, Florida. Produced by Jon W. Reames and David E. Brown.

CONTENTS

NEW BIG FUN

From the sky to the ground
And all the way around—
We can have big fun!
If there's rain, if there's sun,
Let's play with everyone.
We can have big, big fun!

Take a walk outside.
Our world is big and wide.
There are flowers and trees
And yellow bumblebees.
Buzz, buzz, buzz!

(Chorus)

Join your hands with me.
Let's see what we can see!
Then take a closer look.
We'll learn beyond our book.
Look, oh, look!

(Chorus)

1 MY CLASS

A5 & A7 1 **Look and predict. Listen.**

2 Listen and say. Find and match.

A8–9

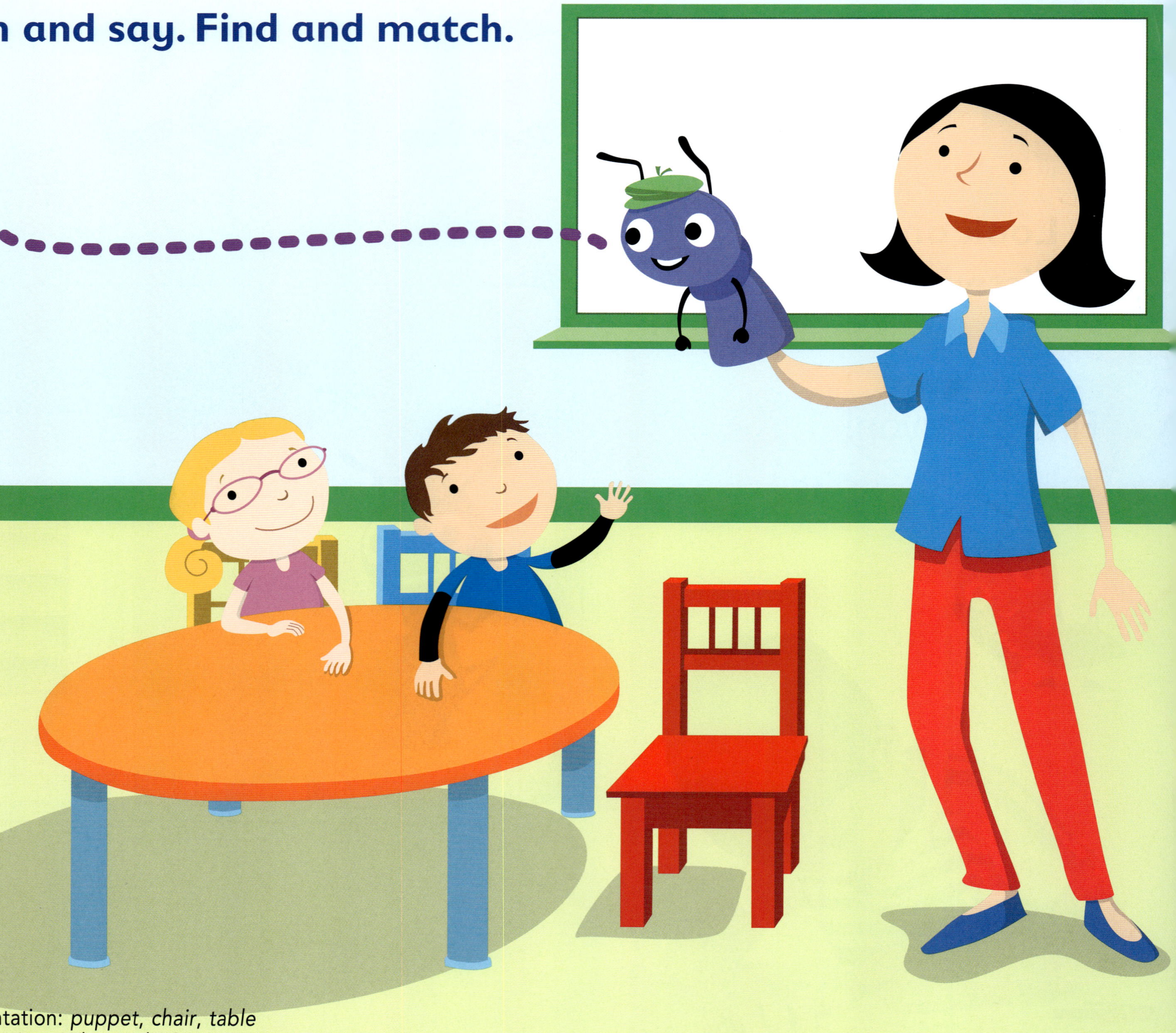

Vocabulary Presentation: *puppet, chair, table*
Language Presentation: *What is this? It is (a puppet).*

A11–12

3 Listen and say. Find and match.

Vocabulary Presentation: *crayon, paper, shelf*; Vocabulary Practice: *puppet, table, chair*
Language Practice: *What is this? It is (a crayon).*

4 Paste press-outs and say.

Motor Skill Practice; Visual Discrimination
Language Presentation: *This is a crayon.* Vocabulary Practice: *crayon, paper, table, chair*

5 Trace and say.

6 Trace and match.

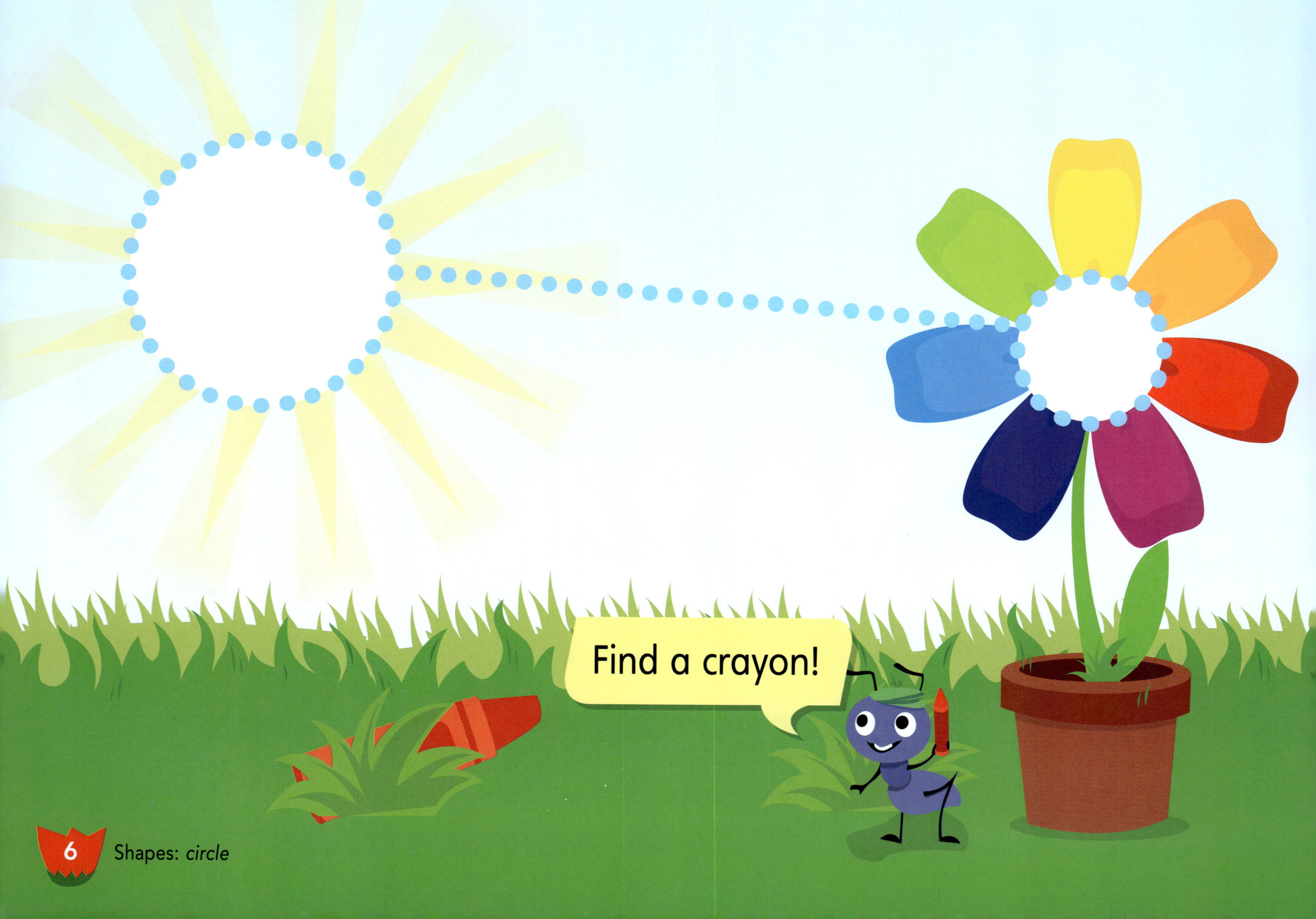

7 **Trace and say. Color.**

8 Color and say.

Oh! It's a puppet.

A17

School Days

What is this?

It is a puppet.

VALUES

9 **Draw and color yourself.**

AMAZING

10 Look closely. Trace the circles.

Amazing: Gardens have all kinds of living things.
Science Words: *grass*, *flower*, *ladybug*

PROJECT

Draw a Garden

WRAP-UP

11 Point and say. Stick and say.

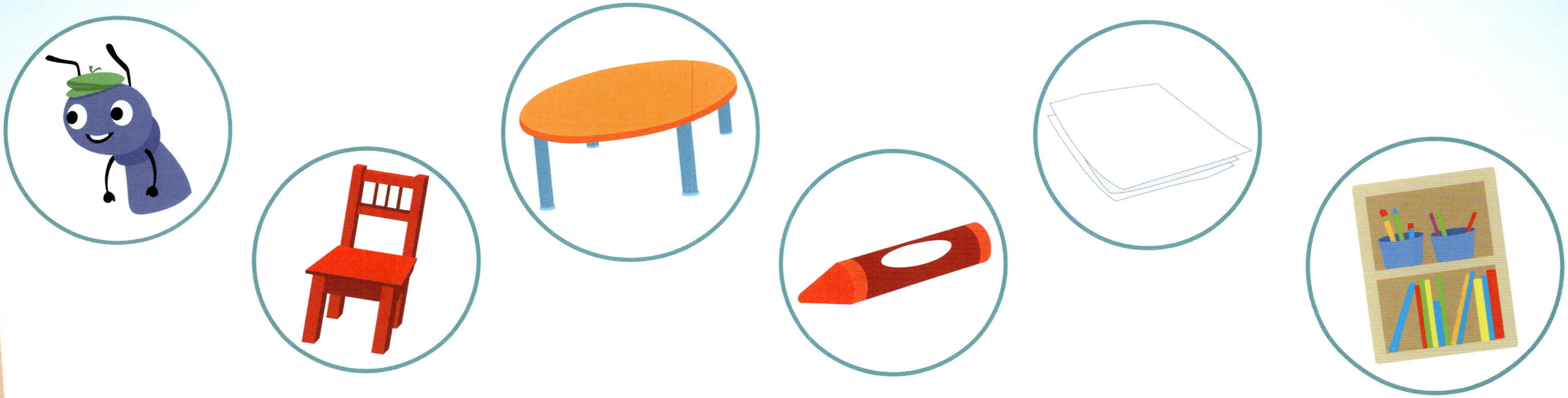

It is a ______ .

2 MY BODY

A5 & A22 1 **Look and predict. Listen.**

A24–25

2 Listen and say. Find and match.

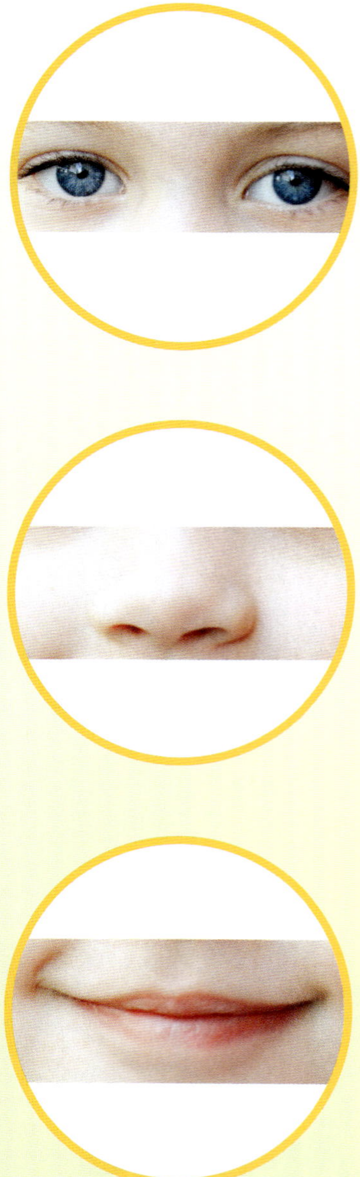

Vocabulary Presentation: *eyes, nose, mouth*
Language Presentation: *What are these? They are (eyes). What is this? It is a (nose).*

A27–28

3 Listen and say. Find and match.

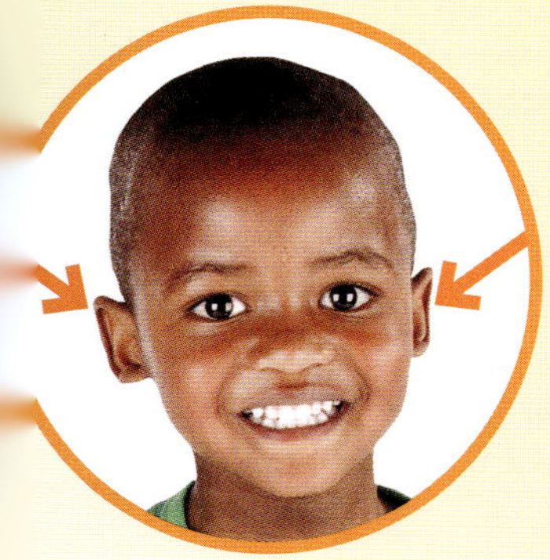

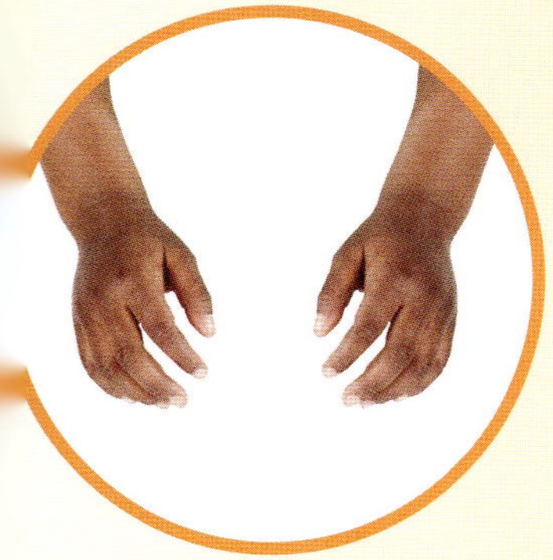

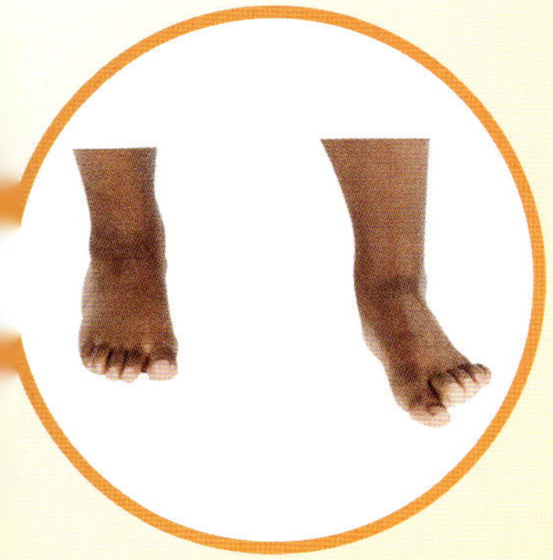

Vocabulary Presentation: *ears, hands, feet;* Vocabulary Practice: *eyes, nose, mouth*
Language Practice: *What are these? They are (feet).*

4 Paste press-outs and say.

Motor Skill Practice; Visual Discrimination
Vocabulary Presentation: *happy*, *sad*; Vocabulary Practice: *nose*, *feet*, *ears*, *eyes*, *hands*, *mouth*

5 Trace and say.

6 Trace and match.

7 Color and trace. Then match.

Motor Skill Practice: Visual Discrimination
Vocabulary Presentation: *butterfly, bird, wings, fly*

8 Color and say.

Color: *yellow*
Review: *red*

It is a face!

A32

What Is This?

What is this?

It is a square.

They are circles.

They are circles.

VALUES

9 **Trace and say.**

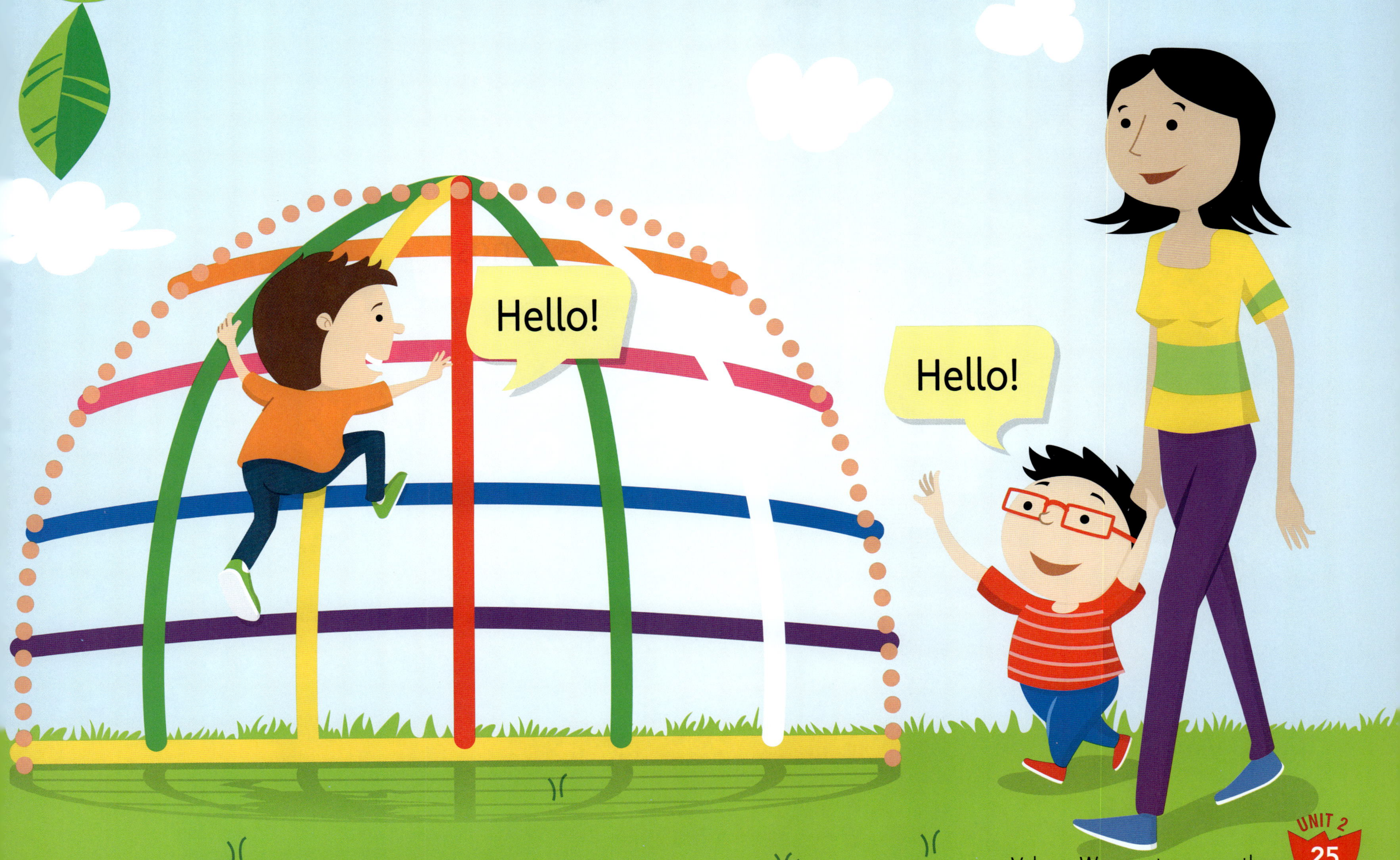

Values: We greet one another.

AMAZING

10 Look closely. Trace the circles.

Amazing: Some bugs have wings. They fly.
Science Words: *bee*, *butterfly*, *wings*

PROJECT

Paint a Butterfly

WRAP-UP

11 Point and say. Stick and say.

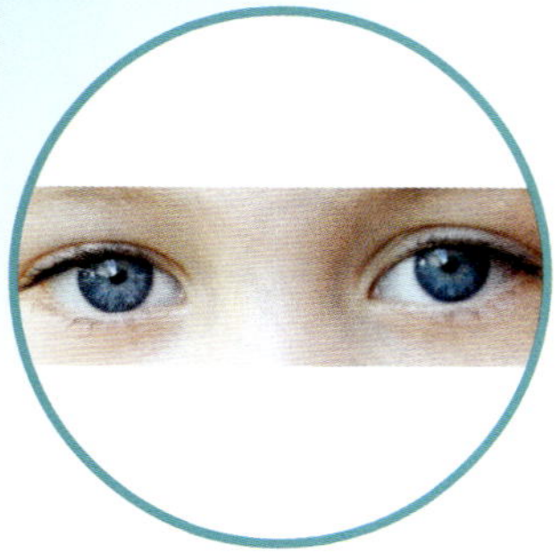
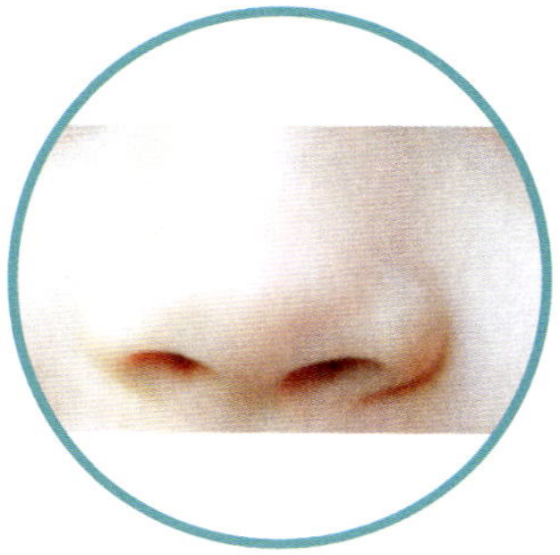
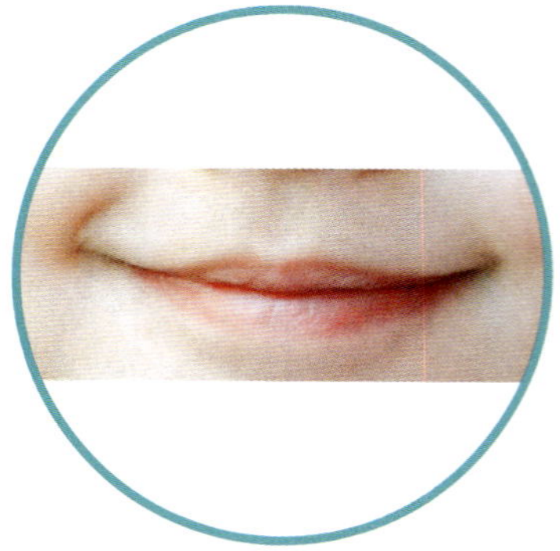
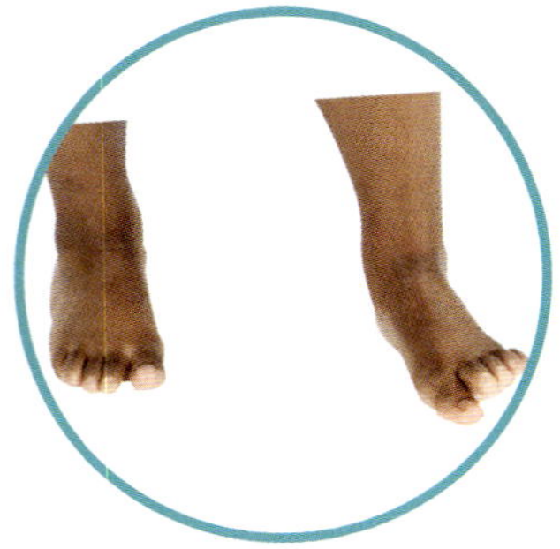
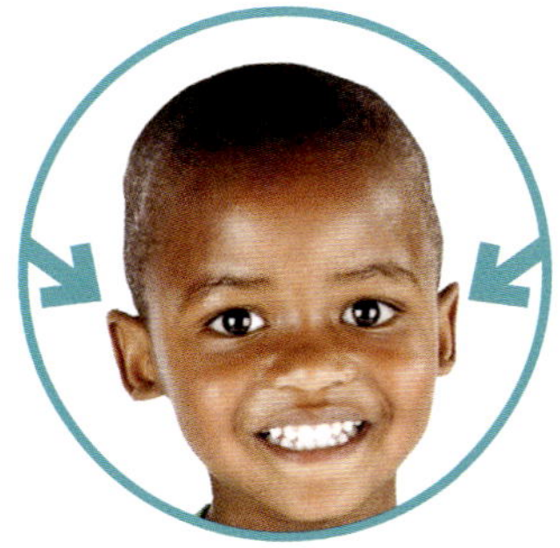
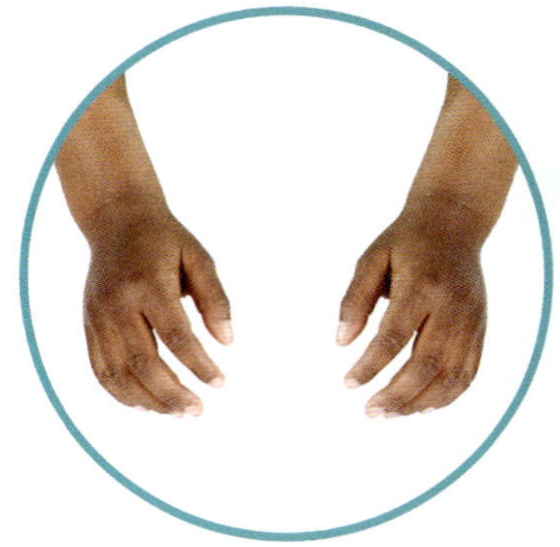

They are ______.

GO TO SHOW TIME Page 117

3 MY FAMILY

A5 & A36

1 **Look and predict. Listen.**

A38–39

2 Listen and say. Find and match.

Vocabulary Presentation: *mother, father, baby*
Language Presentation: *Who is this? This is (my mother).*

A41–42

3 Listen and say. Find and match.

Vocabulary Presentation: *brother, sister, grandparents*; Vocabulary Practice: *mother, father, baby*
Language Presentation: *Who are they? They are my grandparents.*

4 Paste press-outs and say.

Motor Skill Practice; Visual Discrimination
Vocabulary Practice: family members; *blue*, *red*, *yellow*

5 **Trace and say.**

6 Color and draw. Then say.

7 Trace and match.

Shapes: *triangle, circle*
Motor Skill Practice: *Visual Discrimination*

8 Color and say.

Color: *blue*
Review: *red, yellow*

A47

My Family

This is my sister.

Hello!

This is my brother.

What?

VALUES

9 Who is respectful? Color.

Values: We respect others' things.

AMAZING

10 Look closely. Trace the circles.

Amazing: Ants live in large groups and build nests called anthills.
Science Words: *ant, anthill, family*

PROJECT

Make an Ant Headband

WRAP-UP

11 Point and say. Stick and say.

This is my ________ .

4 MY TOYS

A5 & A51

1 **Look and predict. Listen.**

A52–53

2 Listen and say. Find and match.

Vocabulary Presentation: *doll, car, truck*
Language Presentation: *What do you want? I want (a car), please.*

A55–56

3 Listen and say. Find and match.

Vocabulary Presentation: *teddy bear, airplane, ball*; Vocabulary Practice: *doll, car, truck*
Language Practice: *What do you want? I want (a ball), please.*

4 Paste press-outs and say.

5 Trace and say.

6 Trace and say. Then match.

Shapes: *rectangle*
Feelings: *sleepy*

A61

7 Trace and count. Draw 1 thing.

8 Color and say.

Color: *green*
Review: *red, yellow, blue*

We have BIG baby dolls!

A62

Dollhouse

I want dolls.

Let's find dolls.

Look!

Yay!

This is the mother!

I want a doll family!

VALUES

9 **Color and say.**

Values: We share.
Vocabulary Practice: *doll, truck*

AMAZING

10 Look closely. Trace the circle.

Amazing: Wind moves plants and trees.
Science Word: *wind*

PROJECT Make a Wind Toy

WRAP-UP

11 Point and say. Stick and say.

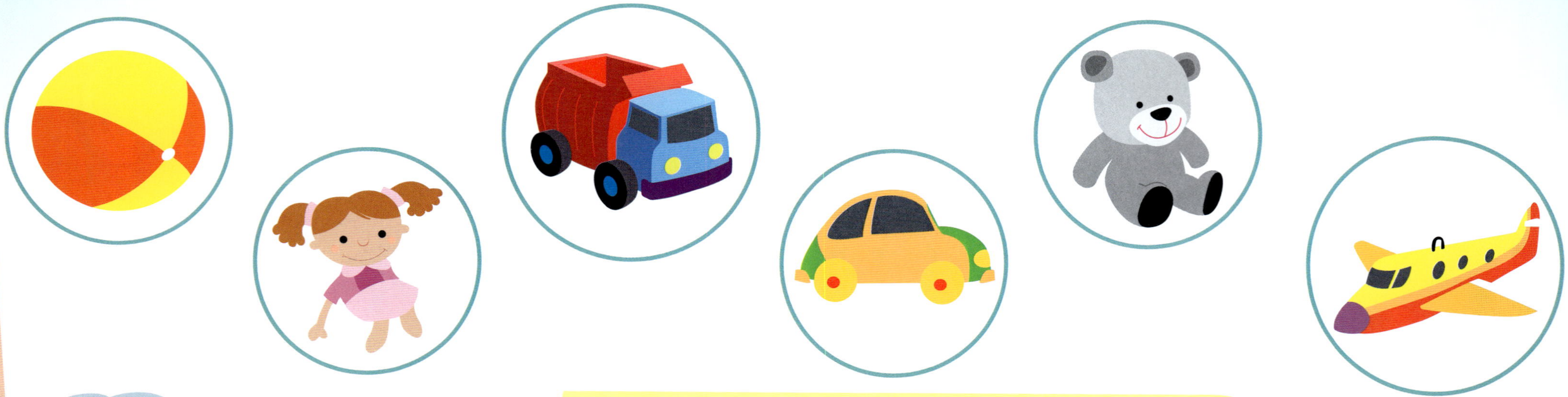

I want a ______, please.

5 MY LUNCH

A5&B2

1 Look and predict. Listen.

Find a cookie!

Unit Preview; **FIND IT** in the unit: *cookie*

B3–4

2 Listen and say. Find and match.

Vocabulary Presentation: *sandwich, lemonade, apple*
Language Presentation: *What do you have? I have (a sandwich).*

B5–6

3 Listen and say. Find and match.

Vocabulary Presentation: *cookie, carrot, milk*; Vocabulary Practice: *sandwich, lemonade, apple*
Language Practice: *What do you have? I have (carrots).*

4 Paste press-outs and say.

Motor Skill Practice; Sequencing
Language Presentation: *Do you like (milk)? Yes./No.* Vocabulary Presentation: *bananas*; Vocabulary Practice: *milk, cookies, lemonade*

5 Find and color ● ■ ▲ ▬. Say.

Practice Shapes: *circle, square, triangle, rectangle*
FIND IT: *truck*

6 Trace and color. Then say.

Shapes: *heart, triangle, rectangle*
Vocabulary practice: *sandwich*

B10

7 Trace and count. Draw 2 things.

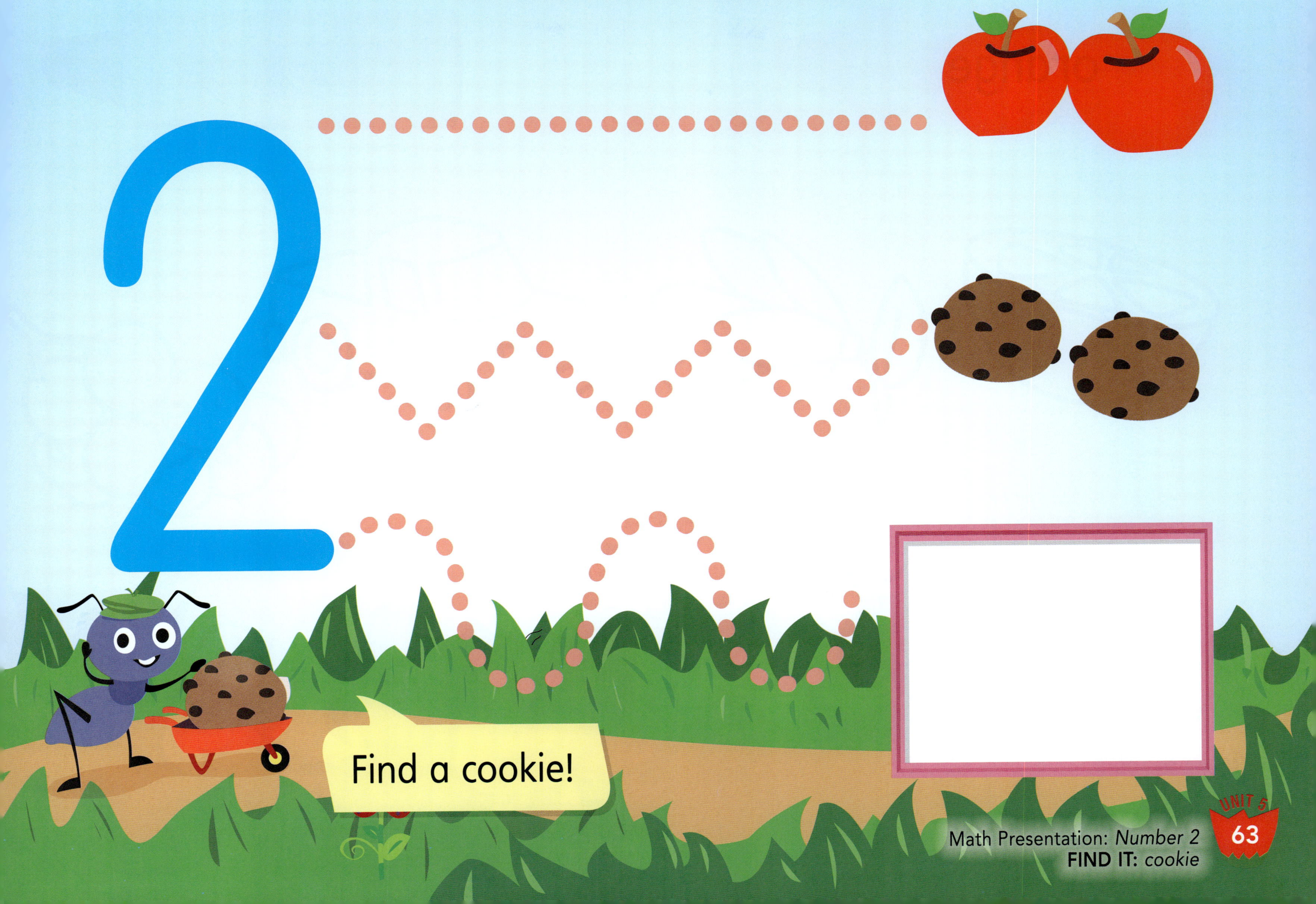

8 Color and say.

Colors: *orange* and *purple*
Review: *red, yellow, blue, green*

We have lunch and
. . . a surprise!

B11

A Surprise

I have milk.

I have carrots.

What do YOU have?

VALUES

9 Color the faces.

Values: We try new things.

AMAZING

10 Look closely. Trace the circles.

Amazing: Some food grows on trees; other food grows in the ground.
Science Words: *lemon tree, lemon, carrot*

PROJECT

Make Lemonade

WRAP-UP

11 Point and say. Stick and say.

I have a ________ .

GO TO SHOW TIME Page 120

6 MY CLOTHES

A5&B14

1 **Look and predict. Listen.**

Unit Preview; **FIND IT** in the unit: *shoes*

B15–16

2 Listen and say. Find and match.

Vocabulary Presentation: *pants, skirt, sweater*
Language Presentation: *What do you want? I want (a skirt), please.*

B17–18

3 Listen and say. Find and match.

Vocabulary Presentation: *shoes, socks, T-shirt*; Vocabulary Practice: *pants, skirt, sweater*
Language Practice: *What do you want? I want (a T-shirt), please.*

4 Paste press-outs and say.

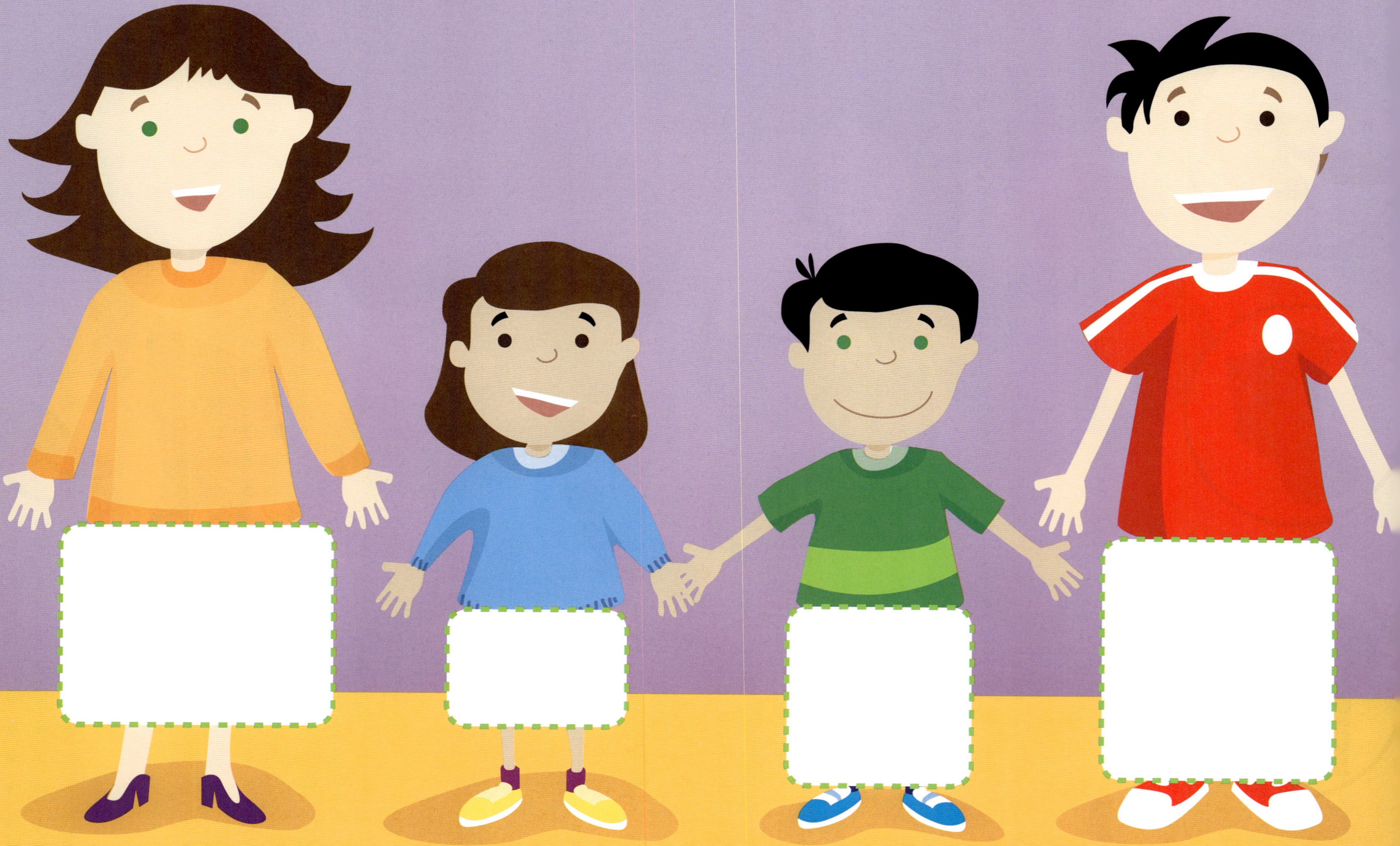

Motor Skill Practice; Visual Discrimination
Vocabulary Presentation: *This is a (skirt). It is (purple). These are (pants). They are (blue).* Vocabulary Practice: clothing; colors

5 **Trace and count. Draw 1 thing.**

1

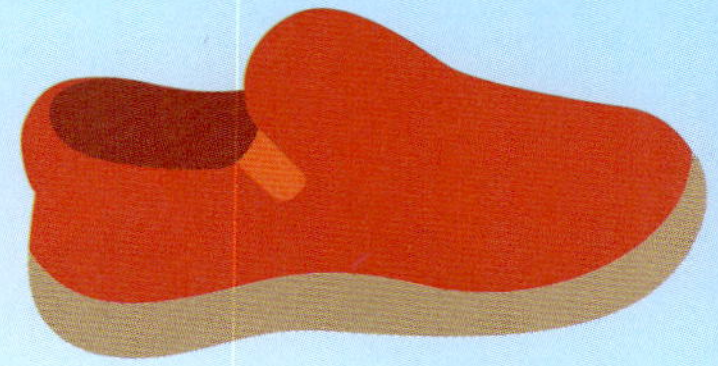

Find a teddy bear!

B22

6 Trace and count. Draw 3 things.

Math Presentation: *Number three*
FIND IT: *apple*

7 Count and say. Then circle.

1

2

3

8 Color and say.

I want a picture, please!

B25

Let's Play

Let's play.

Yes! Yes!

I want it.
No! I want it!

Look at YOU!

VALUES

9 Help the boy find his shoes. Circle them.

Values: We help each other.
Vocabulary Practice: *T-shirt*, *pants*, *sweater*, *shoes*

AMAZING

10 Look closely. Trace the circles.

Amazing: Rain makes animals and plants wet.
Science Words: *wet, raindrop*

PROJECT

Make Rain in a Jar

WRAP-UP

11 Point and say. Stick and say.

I want [   ], please.

7 ANIMALS

A5&B29

1 **Look and predict. Listen.**

B30–31

2 Listen and say. Find and match.

Vocabulary Presentation: *bird, fish, cat*
Language Presentation: *What do you see? I see a (fish).*

B32–33 3

Listen and say. Find and match.

Vocabulary Presentation: *dog, puppy, kitten*; Vocabulary Practice: *bird, fish, cat*
Language Practice: *What do you see? I see a (puppy).*

4 Paste press-outs and say.

Motor Skill Practice; Visual Discrimination
Language Presentation: *It is (big)*. Vocabulary Presentation: *big, small*; Vocabulary Practice: *dog, bird*

5 **Trace and count. Draw 2 things.**

2

Find a ball!

Math Presentation: *Number 2*
Vocabulary Practice: *puppy, kitten*; **FIND IT:** *ball*

6 Count and trace. Then match.

1

2

3

Math Connection: *Review 1, 2, 3*
Vocabulary Practice: *dog, puppy, cat, kitten, fish, in front, behind*

B35

7 Count and find. Then trace.

8 Color and say.

Colors: *black and white*
Review: *red, yellow, blue, green, orange, purple, brown, pink*

I see Lucy. I see her new puppies, too!

B38

Where's Lucy?

Where's Lucy?

I don't know.

I see a crayon.

I see a fish, but where's Lucy?

VALUES

9 Trace and say.

Values: We take care of pets.
Vocabulary Practice: *fish*, *cat*

Amazing: A worm moves without legs or feet.
Science Words: *bug*, *dirt*, *worm*

PROJECT Make Worm Pictures

WRAP-UP

11 Point and say. Stick and say.

I see a ________ .

8 MY WORLD

A5&B42

1 Look and predict. Listen.

B43–44

2 Listen and say. Find and match.

Vocabulary Presentation: *firefighter, police officer, bus driver*
Language Presentation: *How many (firefighters) do you see? I see (two firefighters).*

B45–46 3 Listen and say. Find and match.

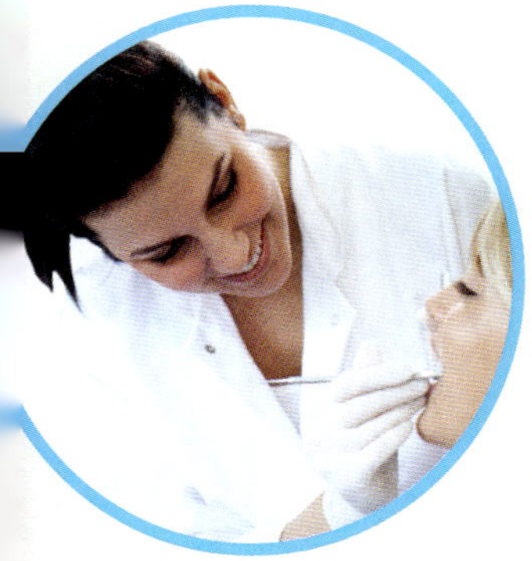

Vocabulary Presentation: *dentist, doctor, nurse*; Vocabulary Practice: *firefighter, police officer, bus driver*
Language Practice: *How many (doctors) do you see? I see (one doctor).*

4 Paste press-outs and say.

Motor Skill Practice; Visual Discrimination. Language Presentation: *The (nurse) has (a shot).*
Vocabulary Presentation: *gardener, shot, baton, keys, shovel*; Vocabulary Practice: *nurse, police officer, bus driver*

5 Trace and count. Draw 3 things.

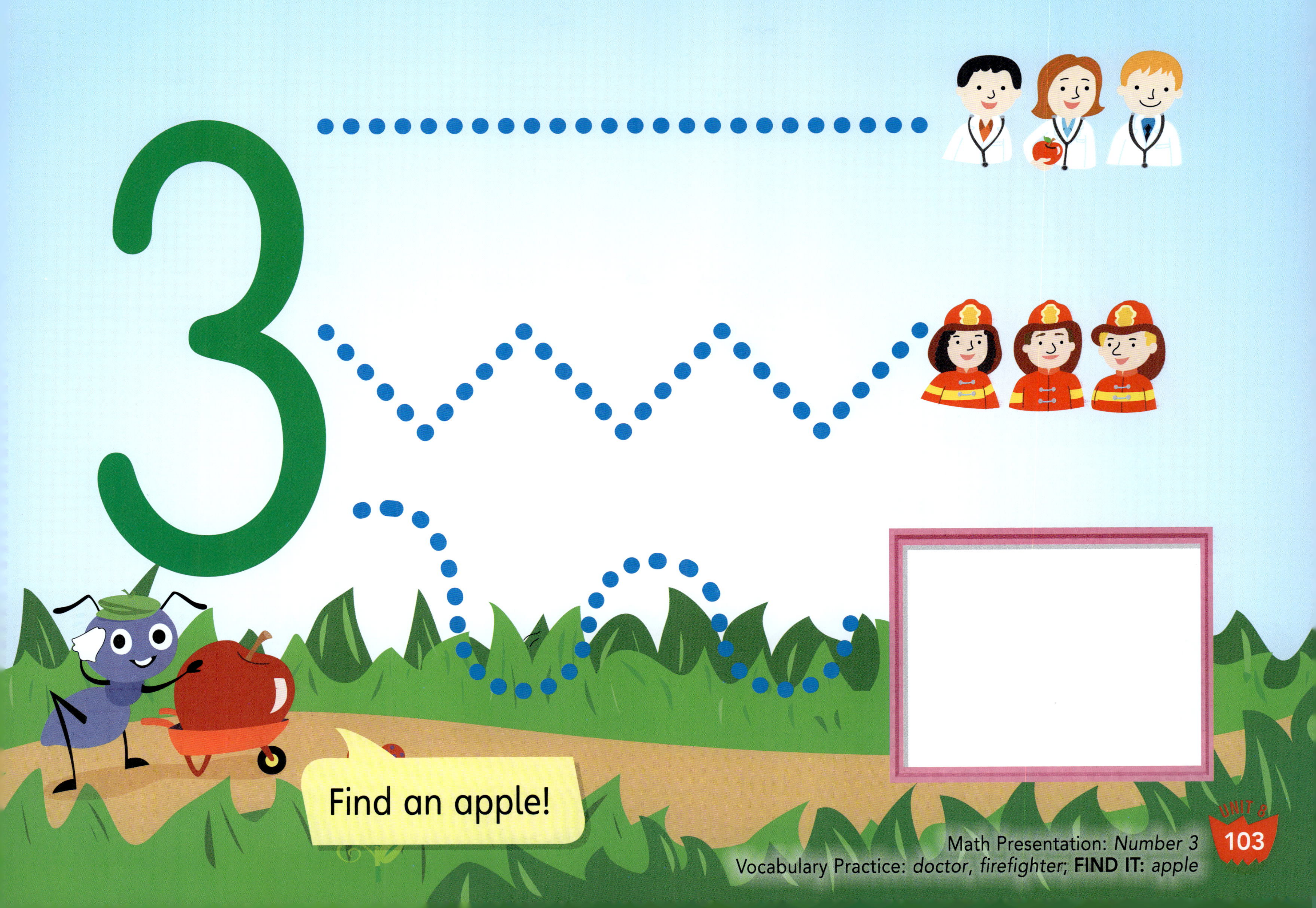

6 Trace and count. Draw 4 things.

B47

7 Count. Trace, then count again. Draw.

5

8 Color and say.

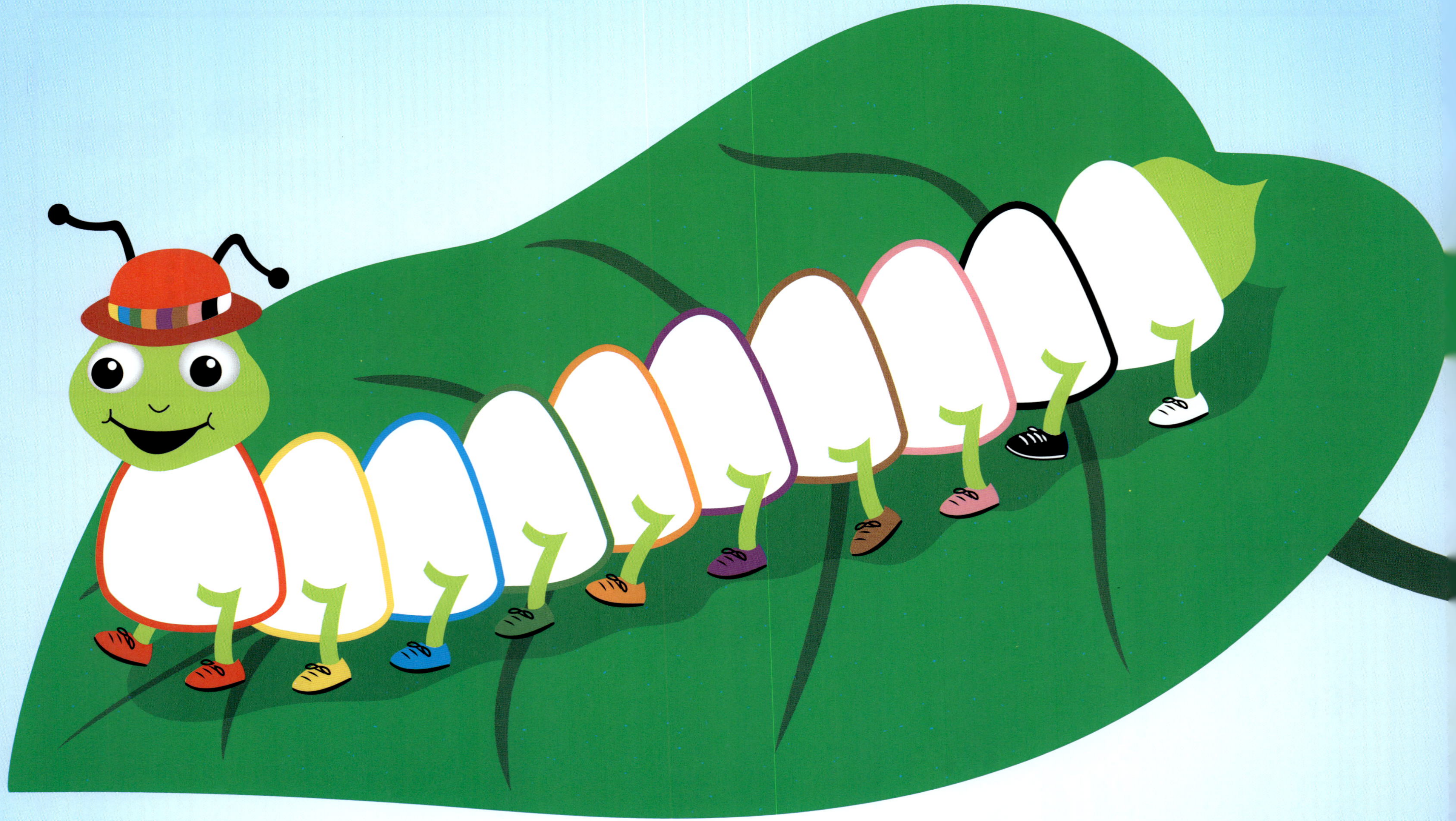

 Colors Review: *red, yellow, blue, green, orange, purple, brown, pink, black, white*

1, 2, 3.
I see 3 balloons!

B49

Hospital

I see 1 doctor.

I see 2 nurses.

I see . . .

VALUES

9 Draw and color the bus.

AMAZING

10 Look closely. Trace the circles.

Amazing: Plants and flowers grow.
Science Words: *flower, bee, grow*

PROJECT

Make Flowers

WRAP-UP

11 Point and say. Stick and say.

I see 2 ______.

9 SHOW TIME

B53 **Listen and sing.**

Unit Preview; **FIND IT** in the unit: *T-shirt*

PROJECT

Make a Mask

1.

2.

3.

 Show Time Project: Make a mask.

PROJECT

Make a Puppet

1.

2.

3.

SHOW TIME

Unit 1 MY CLASS

Draw and say.

SHOW TIME

Unit 2 MY BODY

Draw and say.

SHOW TIME

Unit 3 MY FAMILY

Draw and say.

SHOW TIME

Unit 4 MY TOYS

Draw and say.

SHOW TIME

Unit 5 MY LUNCH

Draw and say.

SHOW TIME

Unit 6 MY CLOTHES

Draw and say.

SHOW TIME

Unit 7 ANIMALS

Draw and say.

SHOW TIME

Unit 8 MY WORLD

Draw and say.

1

NEW BIG FUN

____

has completed **Level 1!**

____

Teacher